IMAGES
of America

CALIFORNIA
HIGHWAY PATROL

The California Highway Patrol's Memorial Fountain lies at the heart of the CHP Academy. Around the edge are engraved the names of all the officers killed in the line of duty since 1929. The fountain was first built in 1979 and refurbished in 2007. The fountain stands as a reminder of the CHP oath to "lay down my life rather than swerve from the path of duty."

ON THE COVER: The Bay Bridge squad is inspected on the west end of the San Francisco–Oakland Bay Bridge. The inspectors are, from left to right, E. Raymond Cato, chief of the California Highway Patrol; A. J. Ford, district inspector; Capt. Rudolph Schmoke; and Capt. A. Paquette. At this time, Cato, as chief of the highway patrol, was the highest-ranking member. Captain Schmoke was president of the California Association of Highway Patrolmen in 1933. The Bay Bridge opened on November 12, 1936, six months before its more famous sister, the Golden Gate Bridge.

IMAGES
of America

CALIFORNIA
HIGHWAY PATROL

Rick Mattos
Foreword by Erik Estrada

ARCADIA
PUBLISHING

Published by Arcadia Publishing
Charleston, South Carolina

Printed in the United States of America

Library of Congress Catalog Card Number: 2007936584

For all general information contact Arcadia Publishing at:
Telephone 843-853-2070
Fax 843-853-0044
E-mail sales@arcadiapublishing.com
For customer service and orders:
Toll-Free 1-888-313-2665

Visit us on the Internet at www.arcadiapublishing.com

To the 210, may they never be forgotten.

CONTENTS

Acknowledgments   6

Foreword   7

1.   The Birth of the California Highway Patrol   9

2.   Academy Life   29

3.   Routine Patrol   49

4.   Quick Response   109

5.   The 210   123

ACKNOWLEDGMENTS

First and foremost, I thank my wife, Spider, for encouraging me every step of the way in all my endeavors. I also would like to thank my son, Ryan, for showing me it is okay to reach for your dreams. This book started with the seed of an idea planted by Caroline Serrato, who was working on her own book for Arcadia Publishing, and John Poultney from Arcadia, who pushed me along. Of course, this wouldn't be at all possible without the help of the California Highway Patrol. Commissioner Mike Brown, Chief Jon Rodriguez, Capt. Troy Abney, Sgt. Jeff James, and photographer Michael Wong greased the skids and provided the pictures. California Association of Highway Patrolmen (CAHP) vice president Rob Nelson covered for me while I scanned photographs and thereby earned my gratitude. I apologize in advance for the misspelled and misidentified captions—old handwriting is sometimes hard to read. All photographs are from the CHP Museum unless otherwise noted. I have to thank Spider both first and last because she put up with the piles of photographs and research material during the life of this project and because she insisted the dedication belonged to the 210.

FOREWORD

It's amazing to think how much California has changed in the years since I played California Highway Patrol officer Frank "Ponch" Poncherello on the television series CHiPs, and it's even more amazing it's been more than 30 years since that show began. You'll see in this book, it's incredible to see how the California Highway Patrol has changed since 1929.

My time portraying a CHP officer was a defining time for me, and although I've done quite a few different acting gigs since then, I'm still recognized by people all over the world as "Ponch." And it fits—in late 2007, in part because of my involvement with another television series, I became an actual reserve officer for the Muncie Police Department in Indiana. It was the culmination of a lifelong dream for me—that of being a real police officer—and one that grew stronger ever since I played Officer Poncherello. I've heard from people in the highway patrol that our show did more than entertain—it actually boosted their visibility worldwide and inspired quite a few people to enter the world of law enforcement. That's always been very gratifying to hear, as I have the utmost respect and support for all the women and men involved in law enforcement.

The CHiPs crew, along with Larry Wilcox (who played my partner Jon Baker—he and I can be seen in our "glory days" on page 62) and myself, strove to create a realistic portrayal of the California Highway Patrol's motorcycle division, but the pictures in these pages tell the real story. Interestingly enough, the department started as a motorcycle force and then diversified into today's modern fleet of cars, planes, and bikes. (And, hey, if you ride, take a look at some of those early Indian and Harley bikes from the 1920s and 1930s pictured here. Those of us used to Electro-Glides and other modern bikes might have had a hard time on those old hogs!) From the early days of the 1920s to modern times, CHP officer Rick Mattos has compiled quite an amazing collection of photographs, including actual crime, rescue, and accident photographs (check out the helicopter rescue on page 114, for example; the crashes on page 78 and 86; or the incredible images of the extreme driver training and firearm testing at the CHP Academy).

Of course, it's the officers themselves, and their commitment to their jobs, that really makes this department. These public servants have given so much for the safety of our growing state through the years. Mattos, by the way, is no stranger to this aspect of the department—he's the president of the California Association of Highway Patrolmen (www.thecahp.org), an organization dedicated to the welfare of past and present officers of the CHP, and that provides scholarship and charitable services to CHP members' families. And the men and women of this department deserve our respect for their sacrifice—just read the story of the Newhall Incident on pages 88 and 89 for a start.

The book includes a poignant note—the story of more than 200 officers who made the ultimate sacrifice as highway patrol officers. This final chapter shows just how serious the CHP's business really is—these officers' on-duty deaths are an all-too-common occurrence in the department, and as with any police agency, the patrolmen carry the memory of these officers with them everywhere. When the book was first written, it was to be dedicated to the 210 officers who have died on duty; that's why that chapter is called "The 210." But in the couple of months since the first draft was finalized, that number has risen to 212. This is one of the realities of the CHP and one reason why I have the ultimate respect for the women and men of this department.

Remember their sacrifices and their stories, and keep them in your prayers.

With deep respect,
Erik Estrada

One

THE BIRTH OF THE CALIFORNIA HIGHWAY PATROL

Shortly after the appearance of the second automobile on California's roads, there arose the need for traffic laws and specialized police officers to enforce them. Cities, counties, and the state's motor vehicle department employed these traffic officers. These early traffic officers mostly rode motorcycles, which differentiated them from the foot cop on the beat. Communication was difficult—a red light or flag displayed on a building signaled the officer to call in for an assignment. These lone officers patrolled the back roads of the state and directed traffic in the middle of cities. They literally used all roads and all codes. There was a need for consistency and uniformity of enforcement so these officers gathered together to form a group to further traffic safety and provide for the families of fallen officers. This group, which became the California Association of Highway Patrolmen, was formed in 1920. As motor vehicle traffic increased, these men pioneered traffic safety techniques and championed the cause of safer roads. In 1929, to further uniformity, these city and county officers were consolidated to form the California Highway Patrol, first as part of the Department of Motor Vehicles, then later as a separate agency. In 1978, the California Association of Highway Patrolmen became the sole bargaining unit for CHP officers.

Harry Wilson was a traffic officer in Fresno, California, in the earliest years. In those early days of automobiles, rules varied from county to county. There were few statewide rules. The need for statewide laws and enforcement of those laws grew with the number of automobiles on the roads. On August 25, 1920, a small group of traffic officers met in Fresno to form a group that would address traffic problems and the welfare of those officers who enforced traffic laws throughout the state. Harry was elected president of this fledgling group. They named themselves the San Joaquin Valley Traffic Officer's Association, changing their name to the California Association of Highway Patrolmen at their next meeting in 1921. The CAHP meets quarterly and is active in passing legislation to enhance safety on the state's highways as well as looking out for the needs of sworn personnel of the CHP.

Here members of the Los Angeles Motor Squad gas up. The motorcycle markings of LACO on the tanks and the shield-type badge indicate this squad has not yet consolidated with the California Highway Patrol. From left to right are Walter Docksteiner, Charlie Brown, unidentified gas station attendant, Sgt. Don Kennedy, Don Graham, and Sgt. Harvey Fowler.

A group of officers, including John Watkins (third from left), shows off their 1915 Harley Davidson motorcycles. Watkins was a Santa Clara County traffic investigator. The unidentified man to his right wears the utmost in 1915 safety gear—leather pants, leggings, and a helmet with goggles to protect his eyes. The bikes are the F-twin silent gray fellow, which sported the new three-speed sliding gear transmission.

In the 1920s, the Department of Motor Vehicles purchased and outfitted mobile offices such as the one pictured here. DMV inspectors would hit the road traveling from town to town to take care of business. In 1929, these inspectors became part of the CHP. Pictured are Earl Chismore (seated) and Art Crane (to his left). Standing at the rear of the truck is Culver City police chief Cecil Truschel.

Los Angeles traffic officer Charles Calkins monitors traffic in this 1920 photograph. He has most modern traffic cop equipment of the day—uniform coat with a whistle on a chain in his pocket, tall boots, pants with leather knees, and gloves. His Harley has a red light high on the left and a siren that is powered by the rear wheel.

Officer Carpenter proudly shows off his specially equipped Henderson motorcycle in this mid-1920s photograph. This view clearly shows the siren attachment at the 2:00 position on the rear wheel; the cable attached to a foot pedal. Stepping on the pedal forced a small knurled wheel up against the rear tire, thus activating the siren.

Pictured are Officers K. C. Murphy (left) and Bernard Isensee They are astride their long-handled motorcycles in this 1922 photograph. The horns jutting out in front of their Henderson bikes are compatible with the lengthy handle bars. These men were the Ventura Traffic Squad. Their only official uniform items are their badges, and their only safety equipment are their leggings.

The Sonoma County traffic squad poses with their Indian motorcycles in front of the county jail in this 1928 photograph. Pictured are officers Shanks, Eberhardt, Lewis, and Roberts. Captain Shryver and clerk Lucille Witham round out the pack. Captain Shryver died on July 10, 1938, after being struck by a vehicle and thrown under the trailer it was towing. Captain Shryver was the 26th CHP officer killed in the line of duty.

Officer Ernie Henderson, from the San Diego area, is pictured here on the far left. His lack of uniform items indicates that this is a pre-1929 photograph. He stands at the United States–Mexico border with two unidentified officers and a stylish woman. The border area was truly a frontier in those days and a challenge to fledgling law enforcement.

These two officers proudly stand next to their well-equipped truck. Inside are cabinets, a stool, warning lamps with colored lenses, and a motorcycle. The lamps were an early form of road flare. The cap pieces indicate that these are both traffic officers, despite the differing badges. Registration on the truck indicates this is a 1926 photograph.

This Oakland Police traffic officer is "written up" by his captain while the corporal looks on. He is astride a four-cylinder Indian motorcycle. This model debuted in 1927 but this is a later version. The siren is mounted on the front fender. Sirens of this type were run off a wheel that pressed against the tire and often activated by a foot pedal.

15

A San Joaquin County traffic officer stands next to a rather dilapidated truck in this 1927 photograph. The hand-crank engine, wooden-spoke wheels, bent fenders, and torn roof makes one hope it is not his patrol vehicle. Is that an evidence tag on the radiator?

With the beautiful Siskiyou Mountains in the background, the Siskiyou traffic squad proudly stands next to their vehicles. In 1927, when this photograph was taken, officers had to provide their own vehicles. A fire extinguisher mounted on the front fenders is an unusual touch for police vehicles in this fire-prone area. Red lights were mounted on the front windows.

The Siskiyou traffic squad poses with their vehicles in 1927. From left to right are Capt. Stephen Kent, Officer Ed Axtell, Officer George Daley, and Officer Ed Belanger. Steve Kent was one of those who made the transition from county traffic officer to CHP officer in 1929. On March 10, 1933, Steve Kent, then 41 years old, was chasing a suspect wanted in three states for bank robbery and kidnapping. Pursuits in the winding roads of Siskiyou can be hazardous. The chase came to an end in the city of Yreka on the far north end of the state near the Oregon border. The suspect exited his car and opened fire, killing Kent instantly. The suspect was later caught, tried, sentenced, and executed at Folsom Prison in 1936. Steve Kent was the 10th California Highway Patrol officer killed in the line of duty.

This is the Kings County traffic squad in 1927. Pictured from left to right are district inspector James Morrison, clerk Louise Thomas, Captain Overstreet, and Officer A. W. Benton. The patrol cars are 1927 Buick Roadsters with ornate radiator caps, and the motorcycle is a Henderson Four with an advanced siren on the front fender. Louise Thomas wears a smaller version of the badge.

Pictured here is the San Diego squad of 1924. A state court ruling said that county funds could not be used to enforce state traffic laws, so officers were under county control while being paid by the state. Cap pieces were all the same statewide, with the bottom ribbon showing what county the officer worked in.

These are Los Angeles County traffic officers prior to joining the California Highway Patrol. L. Kronmeyer, Pat Patterson, Dale Pence, Frank Freeman, and Clint Kingman (from left to right) act cool next to their bikes and a Southern California palm tree. Officer Kronmeyer is ahead of his time with his fur-collared leather flying coat and aviator-style sunglasses.

These 1926 traffic officers pose at the gas station on the northeast corner of Twelfth and L Streets in Sacramento. Standard Oil of New York bought out General Oil that same year, thus the need for a new station name. Uniforms have yet to be standardized. Note the difference in boots, perhaps the most expensive uniform item even today.

The Sacramento County squad is pictured here on February 1, 1921. At this time, there are no uniform items at all, and even the motorcycles are unmarked. The need to professionalize traffic enforcement led to the establishment of the California Association of Highway Patrol (CAHP) the year prior. Pictured from left to right are Walter P. Greer, R. A. Baker, Tommie Ryan, and Ed Schmidt with their 1921 J model Harleys.

The Napa County squad of 1927 cuts up for the camera. Pictured from left to right are Mel Critchley, Capt. Jim Critchley, R. H. Raina, and Bart Freitas. Mel Critchley proudly carried CHP badge No. 1 for most of his career. The Napa squad has long been known for being a fun-loving group of officers.

After his historic flight across the Atlantic, Charles Lindbergh went on a tour of the United States. Pictured here sometime between 1927 and 1929 are (from left to right) Frank Campbell; Capt. Otto Langer; Lindbergh; Blake Mason, holding on for dear life; and Cedric Nielson.

Four officers and their three cars pose in front of the state capital. The cars are identified as Gardner Roadsters, and the officers are (from left to right) unidentified, Inspector George Moynahan, Officer Earl Chesmore, and Inspector Harvey Blackwell. The vehicles are equipped with a variety of red lights and sirens. Vehicles were owned by the individual officers.

Les Manning sits astride his lightweight Cleveland motorcycle. Les set a world's endurance record for a 24-hour, nonstop run on this bike. He was a member of Oakland Police Department's traffic squad when he was injured in a collision. He was loaned out to the California Division of Motor Vehicles and took advantage of his travels around the state to spread the word on the new association (CAHP) for traffic officers. As a traveling inspector for the Department of Motor Vehicles, he was in a perfect position to be a recruiter. A founding member, Les became president of the California Association of Highway Patrolmen in 1927. Incidentally, the current 24-hour endurance record was set by Fred "Iron Man" Hamm in 1937, also a California Highway patrolman. The Cleveland Motorcycle Manufacturing Company was a victim of the Wall Street stock market crash.

Mounted Vehicle Inspectors from the Division of Motor Vehicles are pictured here. This photograph from 1922 shows (from left to right) Charles Reid, Walter Greer, James Morrison, and Frank J. Duncan astride their Harley Davidson motorcycles. The motorcycles had a red light added below the headlight, and the inspectors do not wear uniforms typical of that time. Groups such as these traffic officers from Sacramento became the nucleus of the California Highway Patrol in 1929.

In this 1927 photograph, portable scales are used to check whether this truck is overweight. Notable are the nonuniform hats and the solid tires on the truck. Commercial vehicle enforcement is an important part of the CHP's function. An overweight truck can damage the roadway and become unstable, leading to spilled loads and major collisions.

The same two officers use their set of portable scales to weigh the front axle of a Kleiber truck in this 1927 photograph. The solid rubber tires on this truck were driven onto the scales where the weight that each wheel is carrying can be determined. Maximum weights for each axle are then enforced. Kleiber trucks were made in San Francisco and ceased operations in 1937.

This is an apparently staged photograph of an arrest. It would be very unusual to have a captain and a sergeant leisurely standing by watching a criminal hold out his hands for handcuffs. While the sergeant sternly points to the offender's wrists, the officer seems amused. This could be real life after all.

Pictured in 1918 is Officer Joe Eugene Blake as a county traffic officer. The uniform he wears is composed mostly of a World War I outfit, and his state highway patrol cap piece is a bit tilted. He wears leather leggings to protect his shins. Blake made the transition to the CHP and rose in rank.

Nevada County CHP commander, Capt. Joe Blake, models the new, standardized California Highway Patrol uniform. Rank was denoted by left-sleeve decorations, and the circular highway patrol emblem of the day is on his right sleeve. He wears a Sam Brown belt with a cross strap. Captain Blake endured his career with only one arm, as shown by his single glove.

Conditions for traffic officers were dangerous in the early part of the 20th century. Most rode motorcycles on the rough, primitive roads. Officers were not yet equipped with radios, so when confronting a hostile suspect he was often on his own. Many of the officers from the county traffic squads died while performing their duties. On October 30, 1929, Howard Garlinger became the first traffic officer to die in the line of duty for the newly formed California Highway Patrol when he was thrown from his motorcycle after an errant motorist made a turn in from of him. At that time, soft caps were worn instead of the safety helmets of today, and he suffered fatal head injuries. He had been part of the Kern County squad for four years prior to the formation of the CHP.

In 1927, William Sharkey Jr. took a position as traffic officer for the princely sum of $150 per month. Sharkey was the son of Sen. William Sharkey Sr. from Contra Costa County. In this 1935 photograph, Sharkey poses with his young son Bill. William left the CHP to join the navy in World War II. At that time, he wore badge No. 5. (Thanks to Karl Hansen for information.)

In 1924, Claude E. Swan married Lucetta J. Baker, as seen here in their wedding photograph. Officer Swan was proud of his job as a county traffic officer and wore his "uniform" to the wedding, much like a soldier would in more modern times. A truly standard uniform was still five years away.

Fred Vallejo was the nephew of the California pioneer Gen. Mariano G. Vallejo. In 1912, he was recruited by Mike Brown to be a fellow traffic officer in San Mateo County. He started on a single-cylinder Indian motorcycle patrolling the mountainous roads near Half Moon Bay. Fred's father was reportedly a captain in General Vallejo's army in charge of keeping the peace. (Photograph from CAHP Archives.)

In this undated photograph, Fred Vallejo can be seen running up to make an arrest. The crowd in the background appears to be holding some type of demonstration. Fred made the transition from San Mateo County traffic officer to CHP traffic officer and rose to the rank of district inspector with the California Highway Patrol.

Two

Academy Life

The California Highway Patrol has always been known for the quality of their training, and all CHP officers have attended the academy, wherever it may have been located—the state fairgrounds in Sacramento, military bases, a college campus, and even a hotel. In 1954, the CHP Academy on Meadowview Road in Sacramento was opened. It was a complete facility totally dedicated to training prospective CHP officers. A new facility opened on Reed Avenue in West Sacramento in 1976 and is the current home for CHP training. The academy has several large classrooms, a gym, a range, and an unmatched facility for training for the perils of law enforcement driving. Cadets currently undergo a grueling 26-week, live-in academy, which provides housing and dining facilities. In addition to CHP cadets, the academy occasionally hosts trainees from allied agencies. The motorcycle-training program is known worldwide, and many agencies have had their officers trained at the facility. The CHP Academy also studies and tests new products, from patrol cars and motorcycles to cutting edge weapons to physical performance tests for prospective cadets. The academy is the spiritual home for all CHP officers active or retired with the memorial fountain honoring those killed in the line of duty at its heart.

From February 1, 1941, to March 1, 1941, a class of 32 recruits attended the CHP Academy, which was then located at the Sacramento Junior College. These trainees are studying the complexities of motorcycles and how to troubleshoot problems. The motorcycle on the left is an Indian and the one on the right a Harley Davidson.

July 1940 ushered in 10 new recruits to the CHP. These new officers had just completed an intensive two-week academy and posed with an instructor. Pictured from left to right are Louis Braafladt, Joseph Lucas, Laurance Fowler, Carlos Ramires, David Funch, Percy Corren, Paul Mengedoth, instructor James Brewer, Kenneth Porter, Thomas Lynch, and Walter Swope Jr.

The CHP Academy was located at the state fairgrounds in 1930 and from 1931 to 1938. Classes were held under the bleachers in the stadium. In this 1937 photograph, the underside of the seats are clearly visible as the trainees learn to assist each other in scaling a wooden wall while the instructors look on. Physical education is the toughest segment of modern cadet training, and each day starts with a grueling exercise regime. The CHP recommends that cadets entering the academy be able to perform 50 sit-ups, 50 push-ups, and 4 chin-ups. In addition, it is recommended that cadets be able to run three miles at a nine-minute-per-mile pace, all before reporting for training. Prior to graduation, cadets are required to pass a physical performance test that mimics real life physical challenges that CHP officers may face.

A group of officers stand for inspection at the fairgrounds academy. As is the custom, officers hold their weapon up for inspection with the cylinder open to show it is unloaded. As the commanding officer passes, the officer can re-holster while the next man in line displays his weapon.

Gov. Frank Merriam, in the business suit, assisted by supervising inspector White, and an unnamed chief, review a class of captains at the fairgrounds, which served as the academy until 1938. The stars on the epaulette and sleeve indicated rank. Merriam was governor from 1934 to 1939.

In this January 4, 1937, photograph, prospective CHP officers line up to enter the academy at the state fairgrounds, which were used as the CHP Academy in the off-season. The trainees are bundled up for the cold weather and carry their belongings in a single suitcase.

The cadet class from 1937 stands for inspection outside the state fairgrounds in Sacramento. They all wear the high boots of motorcycle riders. The standard patrol vehicle of the time for traffic officers was the motorcycle, and all cadets were trained in how to ride them at high speeds and in difficult conditions. Car assignments might come later.

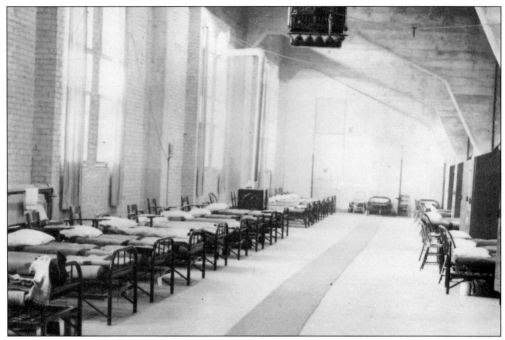

When the CHP Academy was located at the state fairgrounds, trainees were housed under the grandstands. This January 1937 photograph clearly shows the sloping ceiling that was the underside of the grandstand seats. It must have been very cold in spite of the large heater hanging from the ceiling.

CHP inspectors Bill O'Neill (with revolver) and Bill White (wearing the business suit) train a group of cadets in firearm use in 1941. The use of more experienced officers to train cadets is required for cadets to be ready for real life experiences. This group looks like they would be more at home on the set of the movie *The Wild Bunch*.

In June 1940, Sgt. Charles E. McKeen and Sgt. H. A. Durea graduated from a 12-month class in Traffic Control and Accident Prevention. F. M. Kreml, director of the Traffic Institute of Northwestern University, presents their diplomas. CHP often sends members to training at outside resources. (CAHP Archives.)

This is an aerial view of the CHP Academy located at Mather Air Force Base in 1930 or 1931. An early white patrol car is visible at right. The CHP had to relocate at the outbreak of World War II so the military could use the space.

High-speed motorcycle riding requires that officers concentrate on the road and obstacles ahead and not look down. While blindfolded, these trainees demonstrate their familiarity with the controls as the critical instructor looks on. Motorcycle training is now an option for more experienced officers; the training is tough and the washout rate high.

CHP officers are trained in a variety of weapons. They must be familiar with the weapons they use as well as those they may encounter on the street. Sgt. Robert Blossom and his Thompson machine gun train cadets at the firearms range at McClellan Air Force Base in this 1951 photograph.

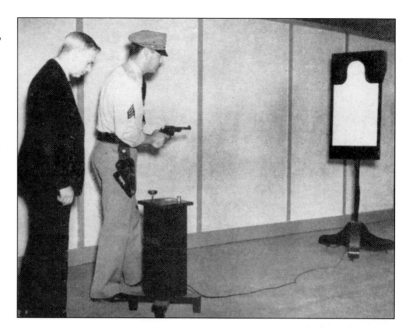

A CHP sergeant tests a "drawmeter," developed to see how fast an officer can draw his weapon and hit the target. The concept was to develop the skill to quickly unholster the weapon, bring it on target, and fire. The target was brought close for the July 1938 photograph, but most shootings occur within a few yards.

In 1937, these CHP trainees learn the proper first aid techniques of the era outside at the fairgrounds academy. With today's training, cadets would learn to stabilize the spine and use a backboard for a head injury like the one shown. In those days, there was little to do but bandage and keep the patient warm.

A group of trainees in 1938 investigate a collision staged for training purposes. Some document the scene, while others inspect the vehicles and interview witnesses. Proper documentation is vital and must be carried out swiftly in an often chaotic environment.

The 1947 cadet class pictured here attended classes at Lawson's Lodge near Lake Tahoe. Money for training was tight, and classes were held briefly in hotels and resorts. In one instance, at a temporary training facility in Placerville, trainees were expected to pay for their own meals in a nearby restaurant and be paid back at a later date.

This is an aerial photograph of the California Highway Patrol Academy in 1955. This academy was located in South Sacramento and was used until the present academy opened. Trainees were housed in the barrack-like structures on the left. The academy had an extensive weapons course and outdoor range.

Trainees practice one-hand shooting at the CHP range. Officers in the field don't always have time to aim with two hands, so trainees practice a variety of strong and weak hand techniques. The heavy redwood screen shown in this 1957 photograph was later damaged in a windstorm and replaced by a dirt bank.

At the Meadowview Academy, meals were eaten at long tables. Academy staff would place large plates heaping with food at one end, and they would be passed down with each of the hungry trainees taking a portion. The skinny trainees were found at the far end of the table.

Members of Cadet Training Class III-58 get motorcycle training at the Meadowview Academy. Pictured from left to right are Jack Campbell, Dalton Baker, Darrel Braham, Jack Burke, and Len Foote. The motorcycles used for training were stripped down versions of police bikes and often took abuse as the trainees learned the tricks of enforcement driving.

This is an artist's conception of a proposed CHP Academy located in the West Sacramento area. Driving onto the academy grounds, a traffic circle is found, which drops out right in front of the main administrative building. Behind the administration building is the quad flanked by buildings. The cafeteria and food preparation facility is on the right, and a structure housing classrooms of various sizes is on the left. To the rear is a recreation facility, gym, and water tank used to train cadets for water rescues and aircraft crews for escape techniques in the event of an emergency water landing. Dormitories extend from either side of this area to accommodate up to 408 students. In the distance is the shooting range, flanked by the high-speed track, skid pan, and road grid. This academy was eventually built and opened in 1976. It is currently used to train cadets for the CHP and some allied agencies.

CHP offices are scattered throughout the state, which challenges the academy staff in providing current, statewide training. They often provide films that send a consistent message to every office. In this April 1958 photograph, cameraman H. Lehman tapes a traffic stop for a training film. Sending the same message to everyone in training is vital in spreading and interpreting policies.

A group of motor trainees circle the track at the Meadowview academy in this photograph from October 1965. Agencies from all over the world send their officers to the CHP Academy for some of the toughest training available. One large agency purportedly quit sending its officers because too many of them failed and they wanted an easier course.

This unidentified cadet from Cadet Training Class IV-90 learns the proper way to take cover behind the patrol car door and fire a shotgun. The instructor stands patiently beside the cadet. The academy range is large enough to accommodate vehicles so cadets can get practical experience with high-risk stops. Cadets learn to safely handle and use the CHP's current pistol, the Smith and Wesson .40 TSW, as well as the Remington 870 shotgun and the Colt AR 15 rifle. All three are available to officers on routine patrol. Other weapons include Oleoresin Capsicum pepper spray, less lethal shotgun rounds, electronic stun weapons, and the PR 24 baton. Cadets must show a proficiency in each weapon and must demonstrate knowledge of when to use them. They are also taught how to identify and unload a variety of weapons they may find in the field.

Students get hands-on training at the academy's Emergency Vehicle Operations Course (EVOC). Here an instructor throws a hazard into the path of a trainee in a speeding patrol car. Shown here in April 1966, this type of training is still in use. Officers must be aware of and avoid hazards that may occur during high-speed driving.

Even academy training can be dangerous. This car was being driven on the Emergency Vehicle Operations Course when the right rear wheel came off. The extreme driving maneuvers taught at the academy puts extraordinary stress on all vehicle components on a daily basis. Auto technicians at the academy constantly maintain the vehicles to a higher than normal standard.

A patrol car skids out on the skid pan located at the CHP Academy in Sacramento. A polished concrete track is kept flooded with a thin layer of water by a sprinkler system around the perimeter. Bald tires are mounted on the vehicles, which will cause them to lose traction at low speeds. Cadets learn the dynamics of a skid in a very practical way. They are challenged to maintain and retain control of the vehicle when it slides in the corners. By increasing the speeds, they learn how to react and avoid a panic situation. The CHP Academy also has a high-speed track, a testing track, and a road grid to simulate a normal neighborhood. Prospective officers can "chase" an instructor in another vehicle to learn how to conduct a high-speed pursuit in the safest manner. (Author's collection.)

In 1974, the CHP started their Women's Traffic Officer Project (WTOP). This was the first time women entered the academy alongside male cadets. Part of a two-year test, the course was 16 weeks long, and cadets were sworn in as officers on the first day, as shown in this photograph. In the challenging world of the streets, males and females face the same dangerous situations and must be able to physically and mentally handle what comes at them. For that reason, the men and women of the WTOP class were treated equally. The women who graduated with that class proved that female officers could perform equally with their male counterparts. Deborah Street won the shooting award with a perfect 300 score, and five of the top eight cadets, academically, were women. The test was deemed a success and made permanent.

The cadets of the California Highway Patrol Academy Class III of 1973 stand for inspection. Their shoes are polished, their brass is shined, and they stand in orderly ranks. They are expected to maintain a high standard of cleanliness and appearance. Dorm rooms are also inspected and must remain orderly. Cadets learn how to stand and march in formation, a skill that is useful when mobilizing in large numbers such as at civil disturbances. Marching in formation also teaches cadets to act as a single unit. Teamwork will be vital in their careers on the road. Currently cadets undergo a 26-week live-in academy that immerses them in a learning environment. They eat and sleep on the grounds in a dormitory-like setting. Training goes beyond the requirements of California's Peace Officer Standards and Training (POST) minimums.

Two lines of CHP motorcycle officers escort the hearse carrying the body of William McDaniel through town. Law enforcement funeral processions are often well attended by officers who not only want to pay their respects but also know that it could easily be them next time. The public often pays their respects by lining the route of the processions.

On October 6, 1934, officer William McDaniel was called to the scene of a wrecked car in Butte County. A garage mechanic with a tow truck accompanied him. The driver of the vehicle, an ex-convict, confronted McDaniel and the mechanic. The ex-con shot and killed the mechanic. McDaniel then exchanged gunfire but was also fatally wounded. The killer was tracked down by a sheriff's posse and died in the ensuing gun battle. Officer McDaniel was the 18th CHP officer killed in the line of duty.

Three

ROUTINE PATROL

Routine patrol is the basic duty of all California Highway Patrol officers—the part of the day that can be spent just driving around looking for problems and checking on the beat. During routine patrol, the officer finds stalled cars and monitors problem intersections for accident-producing vehicle code violations. It has also become something of an inside joke to all law enforcement officers because often what starts out as routine, turns into something else. Many dangerous felons have been arrested after a routine stop for a burned out taillight or similar equipment violation. The major north-south corridor for California is I-5. It is also a route used by criminals fleeing from one end of the state to the other and is a route taken by drug smugglers moving their illicit cargo smuggled from Canada or Mexico. In 2004, CHP reported writing over 143,000 citations for speed violations on that stretch of roadway. With that many stops, the routine can turn ugly. Routine patrol is also a euphemism for the fun time that may occupy an officer's day. The stress-relieving joking around that every officer may take part in helps balance one's life. When one rolls all roads and all codes one never know what one may see.

The California Highway Patrol is always on the cutting edge of technology. In this 1938 photograph, Chief E. Ramond Cato examines a movie camera mounted on the visor of a patrol car with New Jersey State Police captain Floyd William. In-car video is used today to document stops and provide evidence of violations.

The CHP Motor Drill team awaits instructions during the filming of *Crash Donovan*, which was released by Universal Studios in 1936. The movie, starring Jack Holt, concerned the adventures of a former stunt motorcycle rider turned CHP officer. The movie shows CHP officers being trained while Crash deals with drug smugglers, bar fights, and all the usual road hazards.

In 1940, when this photograph was taken, the California Highway Patrol was still part of the Department of Motor Vehicles, and they often shared an office. When the rush at the DMV counter was too great, CHP officers would pitch in. An Oakland officer is issuing a new license plate in this posed photograph.

Officer Mathewson uses a state-owned camera to document vehicle damage from a collision sometime in 1939. The CHP has long been the leader in collision investigations. Working from photographs, experienced officers can determine the dynamics of collisions. Photographic evidence in court can remove doubt as to the events.

Photographing crime scene evidence is a matter of routine today. Digital cameras can turn any officer into a photographer capable of gathering a record of events. It wasn't always that way. This photograph from around 1937 shows a bellows-type camera mounted on a tripod while a second officer is bathed in the bright light of a handheld lamp.

Frank Ryder and Norman Haled form an inspection team to check the headlights of this truck in 1940. The California Highway Patrol Commercial Vehicle Inspection Program has permanent inspection facilities on the state's highways to insure that truck traffic is safely equipped and that loads are legal and properly weighed.

Standing in front of a motorcycle and a 1932 Chevrolet coupe, this officer points his pipe at the cameraman. He is wearing a cap that contains a wire around the peak. Most caps of this era were soft peaked and sagged around the pap piece. This would be known in the World War II–era as a "50 mission crush," emulating bomber pilot's well-worn headgear.

This officer poses next to a 1949 Oldsmobile 88 with futurism styling. This model was introduced in 1948. The 1949 models featured a two-door version designed by the legendary Harley Earl. Emergency equipment includes the "Mickey Mouse ears" lights and the substantial antenna mounted on the rear fender for the radio. This vehicle was known as the Rocket 88 and was the muscle car of its day. It came with an overhead valve, high compression V-8 engine.

Pictured is the convention committee for the 14th annual meeting of the California Association of Highway Patrolmen. The meeting was held in Oakland on October 17–19, 1933. The convention featured banquets, bowling, golf, pistol tournaments, and a parade. Pres. Franklin Roosevelt and California governor James Ralph Jr. sent greetings. (CAHP Archives.)

On May 26, 1939, local auto dealers held a parade of jalopies in the Sacramento area. In this staged photograph, officers deliver an equipment citation to the driver of this fine piece of machinery. The CHP is known for enforcing those equipment violations that lead to unsafe vehicles causing collisions.

The California Association of Highway Patrolmen holds an annual Traffic Safety Conference. In 1966, officers from all over the state gathered in Sacramento for that year's events. In addition to a golf tournament, the CAHP also sponsored a pistol shoot. Pictured here are officers at the Meadowview Academy Range participating in the competition.

Here we have the cast of the *Our Gang* films being stopped by a sharp-eyed traffic officer. Obviously he suspects Mary Ann behind the wheel of being unlicensed. Maybe he thinks Pete the Pup in the back seat has switched positions with Mary Ann and was really the driver. In any case, others in the cast express their displeasure by holding their noses. The motorcycle is possibly a Henderson with the siren just visible at the rear wheel.

In 1929, traffic departments all over California were just being consolidated into the California Highway Patrol. In this photograph, Lt. Thomas S. Lofthouse, commander of the Los Angeles City "Speed Squad," formed to enforce the city's speed laws, shows off his Henderson motorcycle. Purchasing motorcycles, uniforms, and other equipment was the responsibility of the individual officer.

This photograph of an officer sitting tall on his motorcycle accompanied a December 1940 article in *The Highway Patrolman* magazine about the need to hire more officers. At the time there were 700 CHP officers working six-day weeks. Victor Kellick from the DMV estimated that the CHP needed 3,277 officers at that time. (CAHP Archives.)

In 1937, the California Highway Patrol tested the concept of mounting movie cameras in patrol vehicles to record traffic violations. This concept is common today but back then it was cutting-edge technology. The equipment was bulky but very ingenious. It had the ability to record an image of the violator's vehicle and license plate, with the patrol car's speedometer super imposed in the corner of the image. There were problems however. The first image does show the speed of the patrol vehicle, but is that truly the speed of the vehicle in front of it? In the second photograph, an unsafe pass by the car in the middle is clearly seen but the action is so far away, the license plate is not clear.

Courtland Lee West stands beside his motorcycle shortly after his graduation from the academy in 1942. Officer West was part of a training class that attended the Richardson Springs Resort Academy near Chico from March 1, 1942, to March 21, 1942. In this photograph, he lacks the motor boots, breeches, and leather coat he will wear later in his career. (CAHP Archives.)

Members of the San Diego squad of the California Highway Patrol gather for a picture outside their office in 1935. Flanking the officers are Inspector Fred Vallejo, left, and Capt. Otto Langer, right. The women in the center are civilian clerks. Note the woman in the background who seems to have been hiding behind the palm tree. (CAHP Archives.)

This is a border checkpoint set up by traffic officers around 1935. Each vehicle was stopped as they entered California from Tijuana, Mexico, and the drivers were evaluated for signs of intoxication. Many drivers who were arrested probably wished they had taken the train advertised on the billboard in the background.

This highway patrol motor rider poses on his bike next to the CHP office at the Golden Gate Bridge in December 1937. Even in California, the December weather can be harsh for a motor rider on the bridge. The bridge had just opened seven months prior, in May.

CHP's Motor Transport staff carefully restored this 1976 Kawasaki motorcycle for a 2003 Smithsonian exhibition called America on the Move. Pictured from left to right are Chief Ramona Prieto, Anne Davao, Sgt. Kevin Gordon, Brent Glass from the Smithsonian Institute, Deputy Commissioner Joe Farrow, and public affairs commander Tom Marshall.

Ventura CHP sergeant Les Williams minutely examines his brand new 61-cubic-inch Harley Davidson equipped with the first motorcycle radio receiver purchased by the CHP, in 1938. The radio, an RCA AM radio, was a receiver only. It monitored the same frequency used by Ventura Police Department and Sheriffs Department. Calls had to be relayed through the Ventura Police dispatcher.

In 1928, the San Mateo Motor squad stands at ease for the photographer. Pictured are, from left to right, (first row) officer James Dalzell, officer Leland S. Bond, Capt. James B. Logan, officer James C. Wallace Jr., and officer Chester Kris; (second row) officers Douglas Gilson, William Riley, and John Quinlan.

The 1946 Mercury patrol car featured spotlights mounted on the pillar post, an unusual insulated tethering system for the radio antenna on the rear bumper, and a door decal that reflected that the California Highway Patrol was part of the Department of Motor Vehicles. In October 1947, the California Highway Patrol split from DMV to become an independent department.

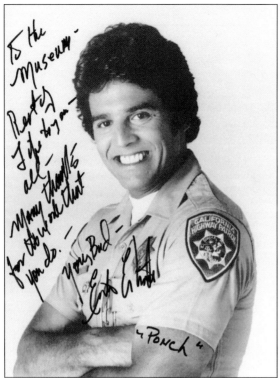

Erik Estrada starred as Ponch in the television series *CHiPs* from 1977 to 1983. His portrayal, seen worldwide, boosted the reputation of the California Highway Patrol. Ponch rode the L.A. freeways with his partner Jon, played by Larry Wilcox. Their characters reflected the hardworking image the CHP has built since 1929.

Television has featured the highway patrol several times in series television. Broderick Crawford, pictured here at center, starred as Chief Dan Mathews in *Highway Patrol*, which ran from 1955 to 1959. Larry Wilcox (left) and Erik Estrada (right) starred as Jon Baker and Francis "Ponch" Poncherello in *CHiPs*. Ponch and Jon's adventures carried them throughout the Los Angeles freeway system from 1977 to 1983.

On October 5, 2007, representatives from the South African government met with members of the California Highway Patrol and the California Association of Highway Patrolmen to discuss California's civil service system and labor relation issues. They also took part in a tour of the academy and marveled at CHP training. The CHP/CAHP are often viewed as a model for public employee labor relations.

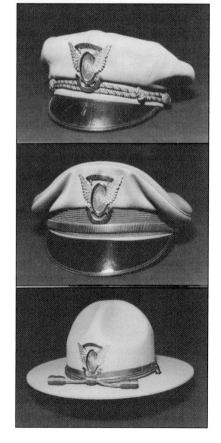

The evolution of the CHP uniform cap is pictured here. The top cap was worn by both motorcycle officers and those assigned to cars from 1929 to 1957. The middle cap was worn from 1957 to 1991. In 1991, the CHP issued the campaign hat. The campaign hat was chosen, in part, to shield officers from the sun. Statistics show an increased risk for skin cancer for CHP officers who spend their workdays outdoors.

The caption on this July 15, 1938, photograph reads, "The Four Bunyon Brothers." Leo Boyle (top), Clarence Olsen and Tom Joyce (middle), and Al Southgate (front) pose in an unidentified location, possibly North Vallejo. CHP officers have long had the reputation for being the finest motor riders around.

The Solano squad demonstrates teamwork and balance in this July 15, 1938, photograph. Pictured are Al Southgate and Tom Joyce in the rear and Clarence Olson and Leo "Butch" Boyle in front. The caption reads, "We're the boys that fear no noise when we're away from home." The canvas wind guard from the center bike was possibly removed for the photograph.

Keeping tabs on traffic in Los Angeles can be an impossible task for ground units. High above in the sky, this 1970s CHP helicopter can get an overall view of the maze of freeways. From the air, they can quickly spot problem areas and inform the Los Angeles Communications Center so they can dispatch patrol units to clear the way.

Highway patrol officers pose with Gene Autry on the set of a western movie. Movie companies often contract with the California Highway Patrol to provide set security and traffic control while filming. This photograph was taken in 1938, but since Autry starred in 14 films released in 1938 and 1939, the name if this particular movie remains a mystery.

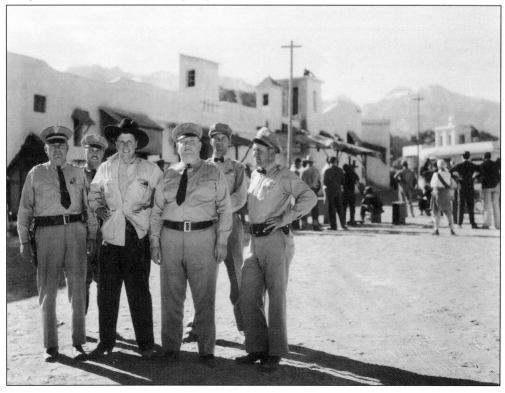

A motorcycle officer stands tall next to his 1935 Indian Chief. Note the leaf spring front suspension. Indian motorcycles had a reputation of being tough, a quality needed on the rough roads of the day. In later years, Indian motorcycles were equipped with prominent fender skirts. The decal appears to say, "Department of Public Works Division of Motor Vehicles" on the outside ring.

CHP officers are often the first to arrive at the scene of traffic accidents. Duties include stabilizing the scene, controlling traffic so no further collisions occur, and caring for the injured. Officers are trained for advanced emergency medical care, with many certified as paramedics and EMTs. Care for an injured child is a top priority and is one of the most stressful situations encountered by officers.

Members of the Marin County State Motor Patrol stand behind their bikes in 1928. The next year they would become California highway patrolmen working as part of the Department of Motor Vehicles. Pictured are, from left to right, officer Burt Reeves, officer David Menary, Capt. Al O'Connor, officer Ronald Hewitt, officer Ernest Monteverde, and officer Jack Agnew.

Officer D. J. Clary from the Bakersfield squad shows off a seatbelt similar to one that saved his life in a rollover collision. Legislation to mandate seatbelts in new cars was introduced that year, 1955, but had been standard in patrol cars since 1953. To help illustrate his story, Clary also wears a parachute that saved him during World War II. (CAHP Collection.)

Officer Rick Mattos shakes hands with then Vice Pres. Al Gore at the successful end to a protective service detail. The CHP provides dignitary protection to visiting heads of state and anyone else deemed to need extra security considerations. To insure their safety, individuals are often brought right to the door of their airplane. (Author's collection.)

This CHP patrol car was used to stop two armed robbers in the San Diego area on January 27, 1941. San Diego police were chasing the vehicle when CHP officers Lester Lewis and Henry Hoard heard the broadcast. Hoard jumped out of the vehicle to take a defensive position while Lewis blocked the road. The bandits were stopped when they smashed into the patrol car. (CAHP Collection.)

In 1937, when this photograph was taken, radio communication with patrol cars was still a relatively new concept. This mobile radio station took it a step further. Station KAPA was built to be towed to rural areas so communication with radio-equipped patrol cars could be established in emergency situations. It cost $1,250, with radio equipment adding an extra $750 to the price. It also provided emergency sleeping and cooking facilities for two people.

Capt. Joe Blake, commander of the Nevada County squad, takes a try at using the new radio system. This station, KAPI, was the first fixed radio station operated by the CHP. It was built by George F. Moynahan Jr. in 1936 with parts donated by Errol MacBoylem, a Grass Valley mine owner.

Traffic officer Frank Dare from the Roseville squad demonstrates the use of a handheld "intoximeter" with the help of patrolman James Hall from the Roseville Police Department. The infamous "balloon test" evolved into the stationary Breathalyzers, Intoxilizers, and Gas Chromatograph Intoximeters and back to another handheld device, the Preliminary Alcohol Screening devises of today. (CAHP Archives.)

Capt. Ed Breuss stands at attention beside his patrol car in 1936. The patrol car is possibly a 1936 Plymouth and has a red light mounted behind the bumper and a spotlight next to the driver. The photograph was taken across from the Willows CHP office located on Butte Street.

With the addition of a 10-gallon hat and a neckerchief, these officers and their captain become cowboys for the 1936 El Monte Pioneer Days. The officers balance while standing on their bikes, and the captain sits on the hood of his car in a show of unity with the community. The crowd stands by unimpressed.

This 1969 photograph shows a California Highway Patrol helicopter patrolling the freeways. CHP helicopters perform general law enforcement functions as well as monitor traffic situations. Passenger officers are rated as paramedics, which allows the helicopter to be used for emergency medical evacuations.

The yearbook for the 14th annual convention of the California Association of Highway Patrolmen in 1933 featured a two-page spread mourning the loss of Les Manning that year. Les was one of the pioneers of the CAHP and had been looking forward to bringing the convention to his hometown of Oakland.

This undated photograph, taken across the street from the Coalinga office, shows officer Jack Tarkington standing next to his motorcycle. Mounted on the handlebars are the added emergency lights, and the siren is located near the rear wheel. The mountain lion is an optional accessory.

The California Association of Highway Patrolmen published the *Highway Patrolmen* magazine in 1937. The magazine was best known for the "Routine Stops" articles and the gory pictures of traffic collisions. Generations of California's driver's education students would, hopefully, learn how not to drive from the photographs. This is the cover of the last issue of that magazine. (CAHP Archives.)

This San Francisco–bound bus rear-ended another vehicle in the Newhall area in 1944. One person died and nine people were injured in the collision. Mass casualty collisions, especially in remote areas, are always problematic. Medical evacuation helicopters now help get the critically injured to hospitals in a timely manner. (CAHP Archives.)

Sgt. Edward G. Stamelos receives the Medal of Valor in 1974 from Gov. Ronald Reagan. Sergeant Stamelos, while on routine patrol, came upon a burning house and gained entry. He discovered the family asleep and entered the house four times to rescue nine children and their parents and take them to safety. During the last few entries, fiery debris was raining down on him. CHP officers are often awarded the Medal of Valor for their heroic actions. Most recipients are humble about their actions, many of which arise out of routine duties. When called to give that extra bit, these officers respond. The first Medal of Valor was awarded to traffic officer Thornton Edwards in 1928 when he discovered a dam breaking and rode his motorcycle like Paul Revere to alert a nearby town. When the water rose too far, he continued on foot.

Commissioner B. R. Caldwell inspects one of the 270 new Buicks purchased in 1955. It had a powerful 236-horsepower engine, a specially designed patrol version. It was tested on a dynamometer to a speed of 108 miles per hour, at which time the tire tread came apart. The Buick Roadmaster is a legendary car still sought by collectors. (CAHP Archives.)

This is all that is left of one car involved in a multi-fatality collision near Castaic in Southern California. The collision, which occurred in the summer of 1943, involved this vehicle carrying five servicemen and another vehicle that was carrying two intoxicated civilians. Unfortunately it resulted in all seven dying of their injuries. (CAHP Archives.)

In commemoration of the 16th annual convention of the California Association of Highway Patrolmen, this yearbook was published. The cover draws a parallel between the current motor officer and the cowboys of days past. The contents included greetings from the governor and the director of DMV and an article by J. Edgar Hoover. (CAHP Archives.)

In an attempt to catch repeat offenders, this system involving 180,000 file cards was initiated in the San Francisco Bay Area in 1945. Court clerks hand searched the files to present driver records to traffic judges. The same information is available today from the laptop computer mounted in patrol cars. Pictured are Jean Baglini, Anne Walters, and Josephine Hahn. (CAHP Archives.)

In early 1940, the big news was the arrest of the Spinelli Gang. They were a five-person mob, headed by "Duchess" Spinelli, who robbed and murdered their way through Northern California. After the murder of one of their cohorts who was talking too much about the murder of a San Francisco barbeque stand proprietor, another member of the gang decided it was time to make a break for it. At a stop at a gas station near Colfax, Albert Ives slipped into the brush to make his escape from the gang that he feared. The rest of the gang continued on without him, and Ives phoned police to report the gang in a stolen car. CHP captain Joe Blake and officer Arthur Barrick, riding in Blake's radio car, caught the criminals near Truckee, made the arrest, and transported the car and suspects back to the Grass Valley CHP office. Careful questioning revealed the truth. Pictured from left to right are Sacramento detective P. O. Emerine, suspect Gordon Hawkins, CHP investigator Harry Hendricks, and suspect Albert Ives. (CAHP Archives.)

On December 22, 1940, on U.S. 101 south of San Diego, a car carrying four people hit a bus carrying 30 people. The car had a bald tire that blew out causing the car to swerve into the path of the bus. The bus drove over the top of the car pictured here, killing all four passengers. The bus passengers escaped with only minor injuries. (CAHP Archives.)

Officer L. Williams from the West Hollywood area ushers in the Pioneer Zephyr streamlined train in San Fernando. The train made a record-breaking run from Denver to Chicago, reaching speeds up to 112 miles per hour! The train was brought to Hollywood, and the Burlington route plate on the front was replaced with "Silver Streak." The train starred in the 1934 movie of the same name.

The CHP booth was a hot attraction at the California State Fair in 1940. The center of the attraction was a simulator that tested the reactions of drivers to different traffic situations. The machine measured how fast a driver could take his foot off the accelerator, hit the brake, and serve to miss another vehicle. (CAHP Archives.)

In addition to the traditional black-and-white patrol cars, the CHP has Specially Marked Patrol Vehicles (SMPV) to assist with enforcement. These vehicles are painted in light colors and have a reduced profile to make them less visible to violators. They are used primarily for truck enforcement. Truckers, with their high vantage point, can spot the traditionally marked units too readily.

E. A. "Snuffy" Smith proudly stands between his motorcycle and a CHP patrol vehicle, a new 1942 Buick Century, in this April 22, 1942, photograph. Buick all but ceased production of cars in 1942 after the attack on Pearl Harbor launched them into war material production instead.

Rescuing victims of auto accidents often means the hard work of bringing them back up to the road. In this 1937 photograph, Officers Howard Amborn, Tony Enos, Arthur Krause, and Ed Baker (from left to right) bring a victim up on an improvised stretcher. Currently, cadets have to pass a physical performance task that replicates bringing a loaded stretcher up a hillside. (CAHP Archives.)

Sometimes the collisions the California Highway Patrol is called upon to respond to hit a little too close to home. The fate of the driver of this 1950s patrol car crash in San Bernardino County is unknown. Although difficult, investigations, even those involving fellow officers, must be conducted professionally and in a timely manner.

Officers responding to the scene of this truck and automobile collision in Stockton on February 18, 1952, were confronted by a grisly scene. Officers had to try to determine what occurred without the statements of the drivers. Physical evidence at the scene along with an assessment of the damaged vehicles helps determine who is at fault.

An unprotected railroad crossing was the scene of this collision on North Tustin Avenue, near the City of Orange in southern California. The crossing didn't have any warning lights or gates and the area was obscured by underbrush and trees. Two people were killed as the car was pushed over 140 feet. The photograph was taken by Sgt. George Peterkin. (CAHP Archives.)

Leo "Butch" Boyle, a member of the Solano County squad of the California Highway Patrol, is astride his motorcycle in this 1938 photograph. The motorcycle has a siren mounted below the headlight and white and red spotlights mounted wide on the handlebars. By turning the front wheel, the lights could be aimed in whatever direction the officer chose.

Construction zones can be hazardous for workers and motorists alike. Late in 1970, this vehicle left the roadway on Interstate 80 in Placer County and plunged into the open construction pit. Officer Jack Wood of the Auburn CHP office investigated this collision. The CHP often sends extra units into construction zones to protect Caltrans workers. (CAHP Archives.)

This 1950s photograph shows CHP officers setting up a truck inspection station. Currently, commercial officers use pickup trucks to carry their equipment. With mobile scales, like those pictured, these officers can change the areas in which they set up, thus keeping truckers on their toes. Their mobility allows them to bring the enforcement to areas that need the most attention.

December 3, 1938, was a wet day in Vallejo. The building on the left is the Department of Motor Vehicles office. The CHP was under DMV in this era. The building in the background is the infamous Barrel Club. The muddy road in the foreground became U.S. 40 and is now Interstate 80.

Actor Lon Chaney shows off his artificial club foot, a prop for a movie in production. Lon Chaney, a master of disguise, was known as the man with 1,000 faces. Here he poses with some CHP fans. Pictured from left to right are Andy Ford, M. Holden, Harvey Blackwell, Lon Chaney, W. P. Greer, and Barney McCluskey.

The officer on the left is checking the headlight adjustment of this mule's eye while the officer on the right checks the "tail" lights. This 1977 tongue-in-cheek photograph shows a Private Vehicle inspection (PVI) lane. The CHP set up random PVI lanes to inspect equipment on vehicles passing through. Proper equipment is essential for safe vehicles. Many accidents were avoided by early intervention from these PVI lanes.

In Cordelia, California, officer Dick Shott from the Solano squad poses with his new stealth motorcycle. Taken as a joke, this 1946 photograph shows that even a hardened CHP motor cop in Solano County can have a fun side. Motorcycle and bicycle safety are priorities for the CHP's traffic safety programs.

On Friday May 27, 1976, a school bus carrying the Yuba City High School choir lost control on the Martinez off-ramp of I-680. The bus went through the guardrail and plunged upside down to the ground below. Twenty-nine people were killed and 23 injured. In spite of their personal horror and grief, CHP officers handled the investigation.

From the 1920s until it closed in 1942, Richardson Mineral Springs Hotel and Resort near Chico was well known for its healing waters. The California Highway Patrol chose the site for that season's academy in 1942. These officers pose over a gorge in the area. Frank Runyon, advisor to the *Highway Patrol* television series, graduated from this academy.

In 1978, the California Highway Patrol began painting large numbers on the roofs of the patrol vehicles. This allowed CHP air units to identify ground units and direct them to where they were needed. During a pursuit or search for a suspect, quickly identifying units is vital. This car is possibly a 1978 Dodge Polara, whose 440-cubic-inch engine made it the author's favorite.

The California Highway Patrol has the responsibility of keeping California's state capital safe and secure, and a large squad of officers is permanently stationed there. Officers patrol by bicycle and horse as well as more conventional means. In addition to security for the building, the safety concerns of the governor and legislature must also be taken into consideration.

The murder of four California Highway Patrol officers in Newhall is known to all CHP officers simply as the "Newhall Incident." It is the biggest single loss of CHP life in history, the incident devastated the CHP and all of law enforcement. After the Newhall Incident, the CHP made fundamental changes in training. Officer safety became the priority in all aspects of every task, and procedures were established for felony and high-risk stops. New equipment was also tested and issued. Because of the CHP tragedy, allied agencies around the world examined their own officer safety tactics and made positive changes. Officers Walter C. Frago, Roger D. Gore, James E. Pence Jr. and George M. Alleyn became the 120th, 121st, 122nd, and 123rd California Highway Patrol officers killed in the line of duty.

On the night of April 6, 1970, officers Walter C. Frago and Roger D. Gore were riding together in the Newhall area and monitored a broadcast of an occupant of a vehicle brandishing a weapon at other drivers. They spotted the car and called for officers James E. Pence Jr. and George M. Alleyn to provide backup. Frago and Gore stopped the suspect vehicle, and both officers approached the vehicle. Suddenly the passenger door opened and Jack Twinning emerged, shooting Frago twice in the chest. Twinning and the driver, Bobby Davis, fired upon Gore, who also fell to their bullets. Both officers died instantly. When Pence and Alleyn arrived, they immediately came under fire. They put out an emergency call for backup and took cover behind the doors of their patrol vehicle. Both officers sustained mortal wounds in the gunfire. The suspects fled the scene with Twinning taking his own life after barricading himself in a home. Davis was captured and convicted of four counts of murder.

CHP officers are called to remove an incredible variety of hazards from the roadway—anything from spilled cargo to stray animals. Drivers swerving to avoid hazards like animals cause thousands of collisions each year. The problem is, once the monkey is removed from the roadway, what comes next?

This staged 1931 photograph shows officers performing first aid on an "injured" woman. Her head is bandaged, and she holds a compress. The officer on the left is either holding smelling salts or offering her a cigarette. Today's techniques are much more sophisticated, and CHP officers have advanced training in patient care up to the paramedic level.

The CHP operates random Driving Under the Influence (DUI) checkpoints, with booking areas and vehicles that contain breath analyzers. The detection and apprehension of impaired drivers is a major concern of all officers, and as traffic is funneled through, officers randomly select drivers for further attention. If a driver shows signs of intoxication, they will be properly evaluated before being released or arrested.

Pictured here is a 1929 Ford Model A. Powered by a four-cylinder engine, it could achieve a top speed of 60 miles per hour. This patrol car was one of the first in the newly formed CHP fleet. It was painted white because it was thought that this would make it stand out from other cars of the day. The door decal appears to have been placed over some other label.

A stalled car blocking a lane of the San Francisco–Oakland Bay Bridge can be very dangerous, and the CHP responds with tow trucks provided by bridge authorities. Officers Herb Lesley and Roy Stallard confront a driver who is obtaining service in this December 1946 photograph. Prior to the Interstate-80 designation, the road was known as U.S. 40.

When called to the scene of a collision, officers stabilize the scene and tend to the injured. Sometimes the injuries are caused by what people have seen. Unexpectedly witnessing a gruesome accident scene can exact a terrible mental toll to officers and civilians alike. This 1960s officer comforts a distraught man.

On August 30, 1957, the California Highway Patrol tested the practicality of using helicopters for law enforcement work and picked the busy Labor Day weekend for their test. Pictured here in the chopper are Commissioner Caldwell and Inspector Cassell communicating with a ground unit. Air units can not only monitor traffic in congested cities but can patrol vast areas in rural locations.

The investigating officer's motorcycle is parked next to a sign advertising the price of gasoline in this April 22, 1947, photograph. This collision resulted in two deaths. Advances in traffic engineering would preclude power pole placement in the roadway. CHP officers look for problems with roadway configuration that may contribute to traffic collisions.

In 1974, the California Highway Patrol began using Maule Short Take Off and Landing (STOL) aircraft for enforcement. The specially designed aircraft was capable of attaining slower speeds while flying and could land and take off from improvised fields. Several times, aircraft in remote areas such as the desert would land on the roadway to assist at collisions or to provide backup for ground units.

Gov. Goodwin J. Knight and his wife, Virginia, visit the CHP booth at the California State Fair in 1956. Governor Knight pretends to take an emergency call while Mrs. Knight prepares to dispatch units. With the consolidation of the California State Police in 1995, the CHP now has responsibility to provide protection for the governor and his family as well as other elected state officials.

On January 10, 1937, these two aircraft were forced to find a place to land in the snow-covered area pictured here. The uncertain surface of the snow led CHP captain Buer to use his patrol car, possibly a Packard, to clear the field for the aircraft.

In 1970, Officers Rice and Wikorski made a routine stop on a vehicle in the San Diego area and discovered the 26 kilograms of marijuana pictured here. At the time, this was the largest seizure ever to come from a routine traffic stop. Officers must constantly be on guard for what they may find when they turn the red light on the car in front of them.

Sacramento officers practice their shooting skills. The picture was taken by a brave photographer who didn't mind being in front of the firing line, on January 26, 1939. Officers train using one hand and alternating between strong and weak hands to simulate real life situations. With only six bullets in the gun, each had to count.

Nelson Eddy takes a break from filming near Tahoe to go for a ride with CHP officers. Eddy was filming 1936's *Rose Marie*, a musical set in Canada. Pictured are, from left to right, Capt. Charles LaPorte, Nelson Eddy in his Royal Canadian Mounted Police costume, an unidentified civilian, and Inspector Milo Hewitt.

Nearly 4,000 people lost their lives in traffic collisions in 2006 in California. CHP officers are endlessly investigating collisions and sometimes they involve one of their own. Officer Dick Wynn was riding this motorcycle when it crashed on January 13, 1958, on old U.S. 40 near Perkins Ranch in Napa. The windscreen lies next to the damaged motorcycle.

Two officers stand beside a 1940 Buick 8 Coupe. The one on the left is a motorcycle officer as seen by his boots and motor pants. His gun belt also has a slouch to put the holster at a more comfortable level. The officer on the right has "keepers," leather straps that keep the gun at belt level.

New Year's Eve is a time that most people spend with friends and family to usher in a new beginning. However, on December 31, 2005, Lt. Mike Walker was working the graveyard shift, and although technically in an administrative position, he chose to spend the evening on the road helping his fellow officers. Mike was responding to calls on the treacherous State Route 17 in the Santa Cruz area when he answered one call from dispatch about a collision. At the scene, he awaited a tow truck with a Caltrans truck also parked there. When an errant driver lost control of his vehicle and struck the Caltrans truck, the truck in turn struck Lieutenant Walker, inflicting fatal injuries. The Santa Cruz officers were devastated by the loss of a man who chose to be a leader on that holiday night. Lieutenant Walker was the 207th CHP officer killed in the line of duty and one of seven killed in a 12-month period.

The Secret Service often calls on the California Highway Patrol to provide officers for motorcades and protect dignitaries. When President Eisenhower visited the state, he took time to pose for this photograph with his CHP protective detail. Motorcycles are used to block of intersections so the president never has to see a red light.

A uniform appearance is necessary, and the CHP has always been noted for its sharp look. Sometimes comfort is more important than policy, though, as evidenced by Officer McCarty from Victorville who dons a plaid scarf to keep the cold at bay. Wind chill is a hazard for motorcycle officers.

Officers practice their marksmanship in San Francisco with the newly opened Golden Gate Bridge in the background. Since California's beginnings, the land in San Francisco near the south end of the bridge was a strategic military base; it commanded a good view of the entrance to the bay from the Pacific Ocean.

On April 28, 1973, a munitions train coming from the Concord Naval Weapons Station caught fire in Roseville just east of Sacramento. In addition to the freight cars containing aircraft bombs were tank cars filled with liquefied petroleum. In the series of explosions that followed, 5,500 buildings were damaged with windows shattered up to five miles away. The CHP officers pictured here witnessing one of the explosions responded to assist.

A contingent of CHP officers lead the way after Pres. Herbert Hoover officially opened the San Francisco–Oakland Bay Bridge. The *San Francisco Chronicle* called the opening "the biggest traffic jam in the history of S.F. A dozen New Year's Eves thrown into one." The bridge allowed East Bay traffic to get to San Francisco without taking a ferry.

Taken on opening day, November 12, 1936, this shot shows the traffic as it was at 2:30 p.m., two hours after its official opening. The photograph is taken from Angel Island, above the tunnel. The lower deck of the bridge also held train tracks, which were later replaced by more lanes for cars and trucks.

Law enforcement careers run in families but the Rogers family had a CHP first—a father and three sons all on the patrol at the same time. Pictured in the academy recreation room in 1983 are, from left to right, Michael, Ronald, mother Lena, father Rubin, and Kevin.

Lee DeForest (standing), the inventor of the vacuum tube, and Flavel Williams, the inventor of the Traffic Eye Camera, are pictured here looking at a camera mounted in a patrol car. The use of cameras in patrol vehicles has been a boon to reality television and useful in court testimony.

Four officers and three patrol cars are pictured in front of the state capitol in Sacramento. This image was taken prior to standardization of paint and equipment for patrol cars. Note the variety of emergency lights and sirens mounted on front bumpers and grills of the three vehicles. Sometimes officers were required to provided their own uniforms and equipment.

Heavy snow means heavy clothes. This photograph taken in 1941 in Placer County shows the extra layers that cold can bring on. Pictured from left to right are Art Barrick, George Hammel, Capt. Charles La Porte, an unidentified civilian, and Capt. Joe Blake. The patrol car behind them is possibly a 1941 Ford.

Opening day on the Golden Gate Bridge found hundreds of motorists desiring to be among the first to cross the straits from Marin County into San Francisco. With the CHP leading the way, motorists pack the bridge. Officer Ernie Roberts rides the far left motorcycle. Traffic today is no different.

On May 28, 1937, the Golden Gate Bridge officially opened to vehicular traffic. California Highway Patrol motorcycles escort traffic from San Francisco to the Marin County side. Newsreel photographers can be seen standing atop the toll plaza in the background. The driver in the car on the right may be exhibiting the bridge's first case of road rage.

In July 1949, this head-on collision left three people dead and three others injured. The collision occurred on Niles Road in the Hayward area and was investigated by Sandy Ankeaskamp and Eugene Muidson, pictured here. Making order out of chaos is a task that confronts all officers daily.

A 1948 Chevrolet Suburban panel truck, painted black and white and with emergency lights mounted on the roof, provided transport for the California Highway Patrol Technical Research Unit. The CHP has used Suburbans and, more recently, a variety of SUVs to assist officers in snow conditions and to carry the extra equipment that is occasionally needed.

Between 1982 and 1993, Ford produced a police package for their Mustangs at the request of the California Highway Patrol. The CHP was trying to find a faster pursuit vehicle in the days when increased emission systems slowed patrol vehicles. Officers liked the Mustangs for their speed and their ability to be stealthy in traffic. Pictured in this April 2, 1983, photograph is Harry Ingold from the Newhall area.

This 1930s traffic officer issues a citation to the driver of the unusual aircraft behind them. The aircraft has a tail, a large aircraft engine with a four bladed propeller, and what appear to be two huge counter-rotating blades above. Could this be the start of CHP's air operations section?

On May 9, 1926, Richard Byrd became the first person to fly over the North Pole in this Fokker Trimotor, named *Josephine Ford* in honor of his benefactor's daughter. The plane then made a tour of the U.S., stopping in San Diego where this photograph was taken in early November 1926. Traffic officers surround the plane to keep the gathering crowds away.

Two sergeants proudly sit in a new 1948 Harley Davidson with a sidecar. A very shiny paint job and lack of wear on the tires indicate this vehicle has had very little use. A motorcycle with a sidecar would be impractical for the high speeds that might be encountered on routine patrol but was handy to carry equipment.

Dressed as police officers, actor Jack Carson and singer Marion Hutton confront a real traffic cop around 1949. The pair toured with Chris Cross and his band, appearing at movie houses from coast to coast in support of recent movie releases. Hutton was perhaps best known as a vocalist with Glen Miller's band.

The Golden Gate Bridge squad poses for a photograph on June 29, 1937. They stand at what is now the toll plaza on the south (San Francisco) end of the bridge. Bridge duty on a motorcycle was made more uncomfortable by the frequent heavy fog in the area. Accidents on the bridge can cut San Francisco off from Marin County and points north.

Four

QUICK RESPONSE

The California Highway Patrol is comprised of about 7,000 sworn officers in 132 different locations throughout the state. These officers all use the same radios and other equipment, and they all follow the same command structure. This allows an officer to work anywhere in the state. In times of emergency, the CHP can mobilize its forces to the stricken area to assist with any traffic or other law enforcement needs. They arrive able to communicate with the local CHP dispatch and with an area office nearby. CHP officers have been deployed to the scenes of earthquakes, major fires, and floods. During times of civil unrest, CHP officers are often the first to arrive, and their training in handling crowds helps restore order. CHP officers have even been deployed to planned events such as the Olympics or other large sporting events. In 2005, California Highway Patrol officers were deployed to Louisiana in response to the crisis caused in the aftermath of Hurricane Katrina. They were housed at the Louisiana State Police Academy and went to the stricken areas in military trucks. CHP divisions practice quick deployment drills and are quick to respond to any natural disaster. This chapter shows a small sample of some of the extraordinary deployments CHP officers have made over the years.

During World War II, threats of a California invasion by Japanese forces were every bit as real as threats of sabotage by spies. CHP officers were ready to handle whatever the war might bring their way. Sgt. Russell Fusion and Jack Costa are shown here with their steel helmets, gas masks, and machine guns.

In 1942, CHP officers trained for anti-sabotage patrols. This officer, using his bike for cover, is ready for whatever may come his way with his M28 Tommy gun. If this were a real situation, he may have put on the steel helmet strapped to his back. Note the fancy pistol grips.

During World War II, CHP officers were California's line of defense against enemy agents, infiltrators, or saboteurs. Law enforcement throughout the state were on alert for agents landed by enemy submarines as war jitters were at their highest. Sgt. Carl Hesterman is ready with his gas mask at his side and his helmet on his head. Hesterman was assigned to the East Los Angeles office.

On November 23, 1971, a Vallejo gas station attendant reported that a group of Hells Angels stole some gas from his station. The group turned out to be 75 strong and responding CHP officers called for reinforcements. The group was stopped on I-880. The attendant recanted his claim and the Hells Angeles were released. The officers involved took no chances when dealing with members of this notorious outlaw motorcycle gang.

The 1960 VIII Winter Olympics was held at Squaw Valley in the Sierra Mountains. The venue was overwhelmed with visitors and extra CHP officers were sent to help with the traffic and crowds. Over 250 officers were temporarily housed at Truckee-Donner High School. This sign stood outside. Pictured are Lt. William Kramer (right) and Dick Graves, business manager at the Meadowview CHP Academy.

Mid-July 1936 saw a strike by the citrus pickers in Orange County, California. The strike was brutally suppressed by the growers and the local sheriff, supplemented by men deputized just for this event. Violence grew on both sides. These CHP officers are escorting scab workers to the fields.

The Donner Pass is notorious for heavy snowfalls. When this San Francisco train became stuck on snow-covered tracks, CHP officers responded to help with the rescue. The snowbank looks to be over six feet high. Seen here delivering supplies is an officer who appears to be talking on a very early form of mobile phone.

In Berkeley, the free speech and antiwar movement of the 1960s saw the CHP called on to assist local agencies and campus police. Peaceful campus protests sometimes turned into violent riots. With batons ready and steel army helmets on their heads, these officers get ready to face the crowd.

On June 10, 1944, the California Highway Patrol joined with the Military Police to man a series of checkpoints along the California coast. In all, 27,000 vehicles were stopped. In addition to looking for drunk drivers and vehicle code violations, CHP officers and MPs checked for draft cards and military ID. (CAHP Archives.)

This is a photograph of a dramatic rescue from a swollen river. The CHP flight officer reaches out to grab the hand of a person trapped on a tangle of branches. The California Highway Patrol Air Operations unit provides emergency rescues and medical evacuations and has been responsible for saving countless lives. The CHP used the Hughes 500d helicopter from 1977 to 1985.

In 1930, the U.S. Army Air Corps conducted a demonstration of how CHP officers and their equipment could be quickly sent to areas where they were needed in an emergency. Their plan was to airlift the officers and their motorcycles in a Ford Trimotor, the state-of-the-art transport of the day.

In this photograph, a rock slide has blocked the road at Rocky Point in the Newhall area. Boulders the size of cars are being jackhammered by crews trying to clear the road in February 1944. The CHP's mandate is to "expedite the flow of traffic," which in this case means overseeing cleanup and preserving the safety of the workers and the motoring public who come upon the incident. (CAHP Archives.)

Temporarily assigned to the Truckee area for the 1960 Winter Olympics, officers had to quickly adapt to the cold weather and snow. Officer Orville Johnson is pictured with issued rubber over boots and long coat with hood. In spite of the inclement weather, he is seen conforming to policy by wearing his tie.

CHP officers with shotguns disperse an unruly crowd in Orange County during the fruit pickers strike. Violence greeted labor unrest in these early years with abuses occurring on both sides. Later known as the Citrus War of 1936, workers demanded a raise from 27¢ per hour to 40¢ per hour.

In December 1937, as invading Japanese forces moved on the city of Nanking in China, the United States gunboat USS *Panay* sailed into the harbor to evacuate embassy staff and other civilians. The ship then moved upriver away from the city and prominently displayed American flags on its superstructure for safety. On December 12, 1937, Japanese planes bombed and strafed the ship and some others nearby. Onboard the *Panay* was Norman Alley a Universal Studios newsreel cameraman. He took dramatic film of the incident and, after the ship was sunk, managed to get the undeveloped film out of China and to the West Coast of California. The evidence of Japanese aggression was flown to the East Coast for development. Special security guards and California Highway Patrol officers accompanied Alley and his precious film, which was kept in a leather valise. This photograph shows Norman Alley and his CHP contingent boarding an airplane to the East Coast. The precious valise and a life ring from the ship are being loaded.

The 1989 Loma Prieta earthquake caused the SR 17 Cypress structure in Oakland to collapse. Portions of the upper deck fell onto the lower deck leaving the injured trapped in the cars. In this photograph, two unidentified CHP officers take no notice of the unstable structure that could have collapsed even further with aftershocks. Their primary goal was to rescue injured drivers.

California Highway Patrol officer Rob Nelson is pictured here with an unidentified Louisiana State trooper on a deserted Bourbon Street in New Orleans. Officers from both agencies joined forces to go from house to house to look for victims of the Katrina hurricane of 2005. Because local officers were often victims of the storm themselves, many allied agencies, including the CHP, responded to assist with rescue and recovery efforts. (Rob Nelson collection.)

Military and emergency vehicles drive through the narrow streets of an unusually quiet New Orleans's French Quarter in this photograph taken in the aftermath of Hurricane Katrina in 2005. After the storm subsided, the enormity of the disaster became apparent. Emergency responders were hampered by endless hours of work and the fact that they to were often victims. Every building had to be checked for the dead, the injured, or those in need of rescue. The rescue and recovery operation was time consuming, but it was imperative that it be performed quickly. The California Highway Patrol committed significant air and ground units to respond to the affected area. The first wave of CHP officers drove to Louisiana. The following relief groups were brought in by military aircraft and used the already-staged vehicles. CHP officers patrolled in military trucks like the one pictured here. (Rob Nelson collection.)

On August 5, 2006, at about 10:00 p.m., Officer Brent Clearman was at the scene of a collision in Oakland when an errant driver struck him, throwing him 100 feet. Observed by other officers at the original collision, the driver sped off, stopped briefly, and then sped away. Clearman died of his injuries early the next morning. The hit-and-run driver was apprehended days later. Officer Clearman had a brief but distinguished career with the CHP. Partly due to his skills and experience in Operation Iraqi Freedom as a marine sniper and his five years of experience teaching sniper skills to military law enforcement personnel, Clearman was chosen to be part of the CHP contingent responding to the Katrina disaster in the Gulf region. Officer Clearman was the 210th CHP officer killed in the line of duty.

In 1989, the Loma Prieta earthquake hit the San Francisco Bay Area causing major damage to several roadways. The upper deck of the Cypress structure collapsed onto the lower deck. In this photograph, the guardrail from the lower deck can be seen just a few feet from the bottom of the upper deck. Many vehicles were trapped between the two pieces of roadway.

Officer Jorry Lee from the Marin motor squad examines the collapsed portion of the upper deck of the San Francisco–Oakland Bay Bridge. This section collapsed during the Loma Prieta earthquake. The car in the photograph drove into the collapsed area in the confusion. A World Series baseball game between two Bay Area teams luckily kept commuter traffic to a minimum that day. (Rob Nelson collection.)

When situations have turned riotous, the CHP is often called to provide additional man power and to assist local agencies. The officer here wears the General Duty helmet issued in the 1970s and 1980s and a flack vest. The helmet and wooden baton date this photograph to before 1981. CHP began issuing military-style Kevlar helmets with the 1991 deployment to riots in Los Angeles.

A squad of CHP officers waits to hit the line at a fire station in Compton. During the civil disturbances in the Los Angeles area in 1992, fire department personnel were attacked by hostile crowds. CHP assigned squads to accompany the fire crews and protect them on their emergency calls. (Author's collection.)

Five

THE 210

This book was originally dedicated to the 210, the 210 officers of the California Highway Patrol killed in the line of duty. The work performed by CHP officers is extremely dangerous, evidenced by the fact that the California Highway Patrol has lost more officers than any other agency in California. The names of these officers are inscribed on brass plaques that encircle the memorial fountain in the center of the quad at the CHP Academy located near Sacramento. On the day after the line-of-duty death of an officer, a bell is rung once at the academy to signify the end of the watch for that officer. Each May, a memorial service is held in front of the fountain, and the bell is rung once for each officer as his or her name is read aloud. The governor, CHP commissioner, and other dignitaries place wreaths at the service. The ceremony is attended by families and friends of fallen officers. Unfortunately, before this book was completed, two more CHP officers died while serving the people of California. This book is now dedicated to the memories of the 212, and for those who will fall in the future.

Pictured here are dedication ceremonies at the memorial fountain at the California Highway Patrol Academy in Sacramento. The fountain was erected and dedicated in August 1979 to commemorate the 25th anniversary of the formation of the CHP. Encircling the outer edge of the fountain are brass plaques. Each plaque is inscribed with the name of an officer killed in the line of duty.

The Academy Color Guard enters the quad at the academy and presents the flag at the beginning of the memorial ceremonies in May, which is held in front of the fountain. The governor and commissioner of the CHP place a wreath on the newly engraved names. In the background, rows of CHP officers stand at attention while spectators gather. (CHP Badges of Honor.)

The California Highway Patrol Academy's memorial bell is unpacked and prepared for mounting. The day after a CHP officer is killed in the line of duty, this bell is rung to mark the officer's end of watch. The moving ceremony is held in the academy quad and witnessed by all uniformed and civilian CHP employees present at the time.

In May, after the CHP memorial ceremonies, another ceremony is held at the Peace Officers Memorial in front of the state capitol in Sacramento. All peace officers killed in the line of duty in the preceding year are honored. As the names of the fallen are read, the family places a rose on the memorial while a dove is released. (CHP Badges of Honor.)

On June 10, 2007, officer Robert Dickey was on routine patrol on I-8 in the Winterhaven area when it is believed he spotted an errant driver going in the opposite direction. The I-8 at this location is generally considered a remote area and a connector between San Diego to the west and Tucson, Arizona, to the east. High-speed vehicles are common. Officer Dickey made a U-turn in the center divider. At a critical point in the turn, a tire blew out, causing Officer Dickey's patrol car to overturn several times. He was flown to a hospital in Yuma, Arizona, where he died of his injuries. Officer Dickey was a five-year veteran with the CHP. Survived by his wife and one-year-old son, Officer Dickey was the 211th CHP officer killed in the line of duty.

On July 31, 2007, units from the California Highway Patrol and Sacramento Sheriffs Department were in pursuit of a suspect eastbound on U.S. 50 near Placerville. The suspect had tried to run over officers earlier in the pursuit and had shown a disregard for others that made stopping him imperative. Officer Douglas "Scott" Russell had just laid out a "spike strip" to stop the fleeing suspect. Running over the "spike strip" would cause the vehicle's tires to deflate and slow the vehicle. Scott had taken cover in the center divider of the freeway when the fleeing suspect deliberately aimed his vehicle at Officer Russell and struck him. Scott was flown to a hospital in Sacramento where he succumbed to his injuries. Officer Scott Russell was the 212th CHP officer killed in the line of duty.

DISCOVER THOUSANDS OF LOCAL HISTORY BOOKS
FEATURING MILLIONS OF VINTAGE IMAGES

Arcadia Publishing, the leading local history publisher in the United States, is committed to making history accessible and meaningful through publishing books that celebrate and preserve the heritage of America's people and places.

Find more books like this at
www.arcadiapublishing.com

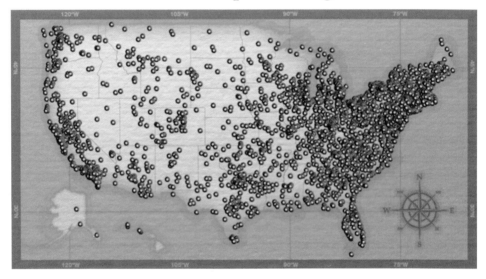

Search for your hometown history, your old stomping grounds, and even your favorite sports team.